Politically
Considered

50th Commemoration of
The Supreme Court Decision of 1954
Brown v. Board of Education

Mahmoud El-Kati

Politically Considered

50th Commemoration of
The Supreme Court Decision of 1954
Brown v. Board of Education

Mahmoud El-Kati

Papyrus Publishing Inc.
Minneapolis • Minnesota • USA

El-Kati, Mahmoud
   Politically Considered: *50th Commemoration of the Supreme Court Decision of 1954 Brown v. Board of Education.*

Summary: This book discusses the impact of Brown v. Board of Education on the lives of African Americans and democracy in America.

Photos: Contact the publisher for details.

This publication was produced for educational and nonprofit purposes.

ISBN 0-9675581-2-3

Papyrus Publishing Inc.
Minneapolis, Minnesota, United States of America

iii

Acknowledgements

This publication would not have been possible without generous support from the General Mills Foundation.

Cover art and design by Seitu Jones

Dedication

For our youth of every creed and color:
A good way to recognize humanity

I know this much about every woman and man that I meet,
as much as I know this about myself.

I know this, I would rather be free than a slave;
I would rather have knowledge than be ignorant;
I would rather be respected than disrespected.
If we learn these virtues, then we have learned quite enough.

What all of this adds up to is quite simply:
Nobody wants to be hurt.

Mahmoud El-Kati

Contents

Introduction

As we reflect on the 50th anniversary of the Supreme Court Decision of 1954, the monumental nature of that decision comes into full view through the insightful analysis of Professor Mahmoud El-Kati. At the heart of his polemic, as he chooses to call it, is an argument regarding the political underpinnings of the 1954 Supreme Court Decision. Professor El-Kati makes it quite clear that in a white supremacist society racial reform always reflects political expediency. It has never been simply through the goodness of white hearts that changes beneficial to the African American population occur. His political overview provides a convincing argument of why this is so. Through a series of assessments tracking the long history of Black inequality in the United States, Professor El-Kati articulates this powerful political dynamic.

It is quite clear that the 1954 Decision went to the heart of the racial structure in the United States. It represented a fundamental death knell to the racial apartheid system of separate but equal. That social structure had formally been put into place in the 1896 *Plessy v. Ferguson* decision. *Plessy v. Ferguson* affirmed the policies of racism in the wake of the Black political gains of reconstruction. Over the decades a number of challenges to this system of white supremacy were mounted, leading to a series of cases underpinning the 1954 Decision. Professor El-Kati contends that the 1954 Supreme Court Decision occurred in the context of the U.S. need to solidify its democratic image in the world, despite evidence to the contrary.

Having set the political context for the 1954 Decision, Mahmoud El-Kati is also quite clear that African Americans have fought and resisted racial injustice every step of the way. He takes us through the history of multiple sites of resistance.

We are able to reflect on the giants and everyday African Americans who have always fought for the extension of democracy – pressing for real justice in deed and not just word. It is incredible to think again of the courage of Paul Robeson, W. E. B. DuBois, A. Phillip Randolph, and the countless unsung men and women who paved the way for 1954. Perhaps the least well known and crucial to this victory was Charles Houston. He is surely the greatest of the unsung heroes in the history of the 1954 Decision. El-Kati clarifies this. Charles Houston was a true giant of courage and determination, training at Howard University Law School a legion of students, including the lead counsel for the 1954 NAACP case, Thurgood Marshall. Marshall, of course, went on to become the first African American Supreme Court Justice.

Professor Mahmoud El-Kati has written an important tract, short and relevant for the challenging days ahead. In this difficult period of plotting the next phase of African American struggle in the new millennium, we have a valuable guidepost in Mahmoud El-Kati's political consideration of the Supreme Court Decision of 1954.

Rose M. Brewer, Ph.D.
University of Minnesota

Foreword

The most *terrifying* thing in the soul of American societal life is the unnamed fear of being honest with itself. Americans have a militant, almost rock-like aversion to certain truths. They unwittingly deny the undeniable. The words of this small booklet make no attempt towards "objective systematic analysis." The content is purely polemical, that is to say, an argument, a point of view. In short, it is an attempt to be honest with oneself, as much as anything else. It is an attempt, to explore raw and unguided truths, as I understand them, with critical intentions, as to the motives behind a landmark Supreme Court decision. It is also an attempt to assess its meaning and value. There is, first and foremost, an insistence here on indicting the demon in our midst that is at the root of America's racial problems, and that is *the doctrine of white supremacy*. While we rarely if ever acknowledge this reality today since the reforms of the 1960s, I submit that this social belief still informs Americans in very powerful ways. It still persistently functions with a life of its own. Until the false belief in *white superiority and Black inferiority* is thoroughly smashed, there can be no true justice, no social equality in this land, and no permanent social peace. *"If you don't understand the doctrine of white supremacy, you are going to be confused about everything else in this society,"* says social critic and activist Neilly Fuller. I, for one, concur.

The current crop of American leaders, political, religious, and cultural across the board, seem to be morally incapable of addressing this central idea of American life and history, the idea of "Race." I dare to proffer the declaration of the French writer, Albert Camus: "Self condemnation is impossible. Man can not condemn himself; therefore, I must condemn." It will not be argued here that *Brown v. Board of Education* did not have a *profound and lasting*, even life-giving impact on the branch of the U.S. Government forthrightly addressed "The Negro question" represented a monumental surprise and, accordingly, a harbinger of emerging discontent. Such positive action had been so rarely effected by any branch of the U.S. Government: Repeal of the *Grandfather's Clause* by the Supreme Court in 1913, two executive orders (1941 and 1948); and in between the Court outlawed the "white primaries" in 1944. These are the three biggest examples of the U.S. Government assuming its constitutional responsibility with respect to Black Americans. The defeat of Reconstruction by the powers of white supremacy on the heels of the official outlawing of the institution of "Negro" enslavement introduced, for the most part, a long nightmare of silence on "The Negro question," a term preceding the movement's more modern term, "civil rights." Both terms, in essence, speak to African Americans, their oppressed condition, and their struggle for full human rights in America over several centuries.

One hopes that the sense of my arguments raises other arguments, in the quest for a true participatory democracy in America. Nothing can be solved that can't be faced. Let it be clear from this quarter, that *American democracy is a work in progress,* not a finished product as too many American opinion makers and callous political leaders so facilely assert. It is nowhere near – to use the oxymoronic phrase – "a more perfect union." Democracy in America remains essentially a theory, not a dependable practice of government. The Supreme Court Decision of 1954 is but a halting, though progressive, step in achieving democracy. The society in which certain people might be relieved of bearing the burden of "race" is unclear; a society in which inclusiveness, tolerance, and respect for human personality, wherein people will learn to live together without having to live alike, is still afar. There is a very silly book on the market, written by an obviously silly and irresponsible writer from an American think tank, titled *The End of Racism*. I did not read it, because I would not allow myself to read it. Such a title, which suggests a trivializing of the inexplicable, unearned suffering that Black folk have endured, and still endure, is beneath the dignity of my criticism. Racism cannot end with the stroke of a pen or by wishful thinking. It will end only through Frederick Douglass' "earnest struggle," by a powerful and persistent movement of the will, a will that must finally and unmistakably smother the inhumanity of racism with a new wave of humanity that claims us all.

Brown v. Board of Education: to what end? The thrust of this modest reexamination is unabashedly exercised with moral overtones – a scary thing to do today, which does not smack of some self-serving religious gimmickry. *Brown v. Board of Education* is most certainly not an end but serves to remind us of what is to be done. This decision, handed down unanimously, represents a tippy-toe moral advance, even though moral advancement in lifting the veil of oppression was not at the heart of the High Court's intentions; in the broad scheme of things the Court did "the right thing for the wrong reason." Old-fashioned American practical politics was at the bottom of this seemingly noble act. This decision should serve to remind all democracy-seeking people in America that every struggle makes a greater struggle necessary. I have intentionally used this, perhaps most historic of all Supreme Court decisions, to discuss a mosaic of issues that are intrinsically bounded to it. Let it be said that everything is related to everything. This is the nature of the complexity of life. Everything has its place, yet everything is related – and there are no free lunches. And hence, the dictum of the British economist, Barbara Ward, "People do not get what they do not want, and they do not work for what they do not imagine."

Mahmoud El-Kati

The Roots of The Question

"Does segregation of children in public schools solely on the basis of race, even though the physical facilities and other 'tangible' factors may be equal, deprive children of the minority group of equal education opportunities?" The answer to that question was, "We believe it does." Those were the words of Chief Justice Earl B. Warren, and the decision of his Court was 9 to 0 in favor of this opinion.

This Supreme Court decision, rendered on May 17, 1954, sounded the death knell for officially sanctioned, racially segregated education in American society. Though the basic aim of this decision was directed towards the dual education system of the deep South, it included the border states as well; a fact that often gets lost in the assessment of this sea changing event. Kansas, more Midwest than South, is often assigned a place as a border state.

Linda Brown

With hindsight, we can see that this landmark decision on the part of the judiciary branch of the U.S. Government would contribute mightily to reforming the patterns of American political and racial history. It was after a fashion the pivot of a then imperceptibly changing America. Then, as now, change to most Americans belongs essentially to the material world. Shortly after the decision was handed down, James Hinton, who sparked the NAACP drive in the key Clarendon County of South Carolina suit, closed his life insurance office and hurried home to "get the Colored people ready." In Virginia, Barbara Trent, 16, broke down in tears when her teacher announced the decision. "We went on studying history," she said, "but things weren't the same, and will never be the same again." At long last, to all Black people south and north as well, a conspicuous burden of racial injustice had been lifted.

The Court decision that outlawed school segregation was the result of cases from four states (South Carolina, Virginia, Delaware, Kansas) and the District of Columbia. There is a story of high drama, labor, sacrifice, and suffering in each of these stories. These little-known people who filed suits against the evils of segregation are the real heroes of *Brown v. Board*. Thurgood Marshall, who was later appointed to the Supreme Court bench by President Lyndon B. Johnson, was then Chief Counsel of the NAACP Legal Defense Fund. It was he, along with attorneys George E. C. Hayes and James Nabrit and other lawyers, who had asked the Court to overturn the *Plessy v. Ferguson* decision of 1896 and declare

(l. to r.) Louis L. Redding, Robert Carter, Oliver W. Hill, Thurgood Marshall, Spottswood Robinson, Jack Greenberg, James Nabrit Jr., George E. C. Hayes, Constance Motley (Next Page)

segregation in tax supported public schools  unconstitutional. The *Plessy v. Ferguson* decision upheld the concept of racial segregation when it ruled in favor of the "separate but equal" doctrine fostered by southern politicians at the close of the 19th century. That decision, in effect, endorsed the terror-driven doctrine of white supremacy. Justice John Harlan, with his plea for a "color-blind society," with "no caste or class distinction," was the lone

Constance Motley

dissenting voice on the bench at that time. He went on to say that "the thin disguise of equal accommodations...will not mislead anyone, nor atone for the wrong this day done." His moral integrity was in keeping with the spirit of the American creed, which challenged the "wisdom" of his peers on the High Court. Justice Harlan uttered those words despite the fact he too, paradoxically, accepted the popular belief in the innate "inferiority of the Negro." Seven years later, the young and brilliant Harvard graduate, W.E.B. DuBois would surface this issue in The Clarion Call as to what was ahead for the new century in 1903: "The problem of the twentieth century is the problem of the color line...."

Plessy v. Ferguson resulted from Homer Plessy, an "Octoroon" who lived in New Orleans, Louisiana, filing suit for the right to a seat of his choice on a public streetcar in 1892. At that time, the unvarnished racist rulers of the South – with the tacit approval of the power elite in the north – were instituting a gaggle of "race" laws (Black Codes). Such laws were intended to completely disenfranchise Black citizens who enjoyed a brief spurt of citizen participation during the Reconstruction period (1865–1876) when the Freedmen (ex-slaves) were granted equality by "The Civil War amendments": the Thirteenth, Fourteenth, and Fifteenth amendments of the U.S. Constitution. They were intended to do three things: officially outlaw a two and one-half century institution of Black enslavement, grant full citizenship, and grant the right to vote to Black (male) people. The *Plessy v. Ferguson* decision officially and effectively nullified all of the social progress that had been made during Reconstruction. The hopes and aspirations of the Black population had been dashed. The promising humanitarian work of white and Black northerners who came south to aid the optimistic Black Freedmen, including a few fair-minded white southerners, was defeated by naked power. "The Negro" had been abruptly "put back in his place."

The die was thus cast. The roots of the "Negro question," (which became the Civil Rights Movement) comes from this background of broken promises. It is grounded in the quest for social justice as articulated by the Declaration of Independence, the Constitution, and the Bill of Rights. Further, and even more critically, this struggle then and now is a moral one. It is not, and has never been simply about politics and power. The African American fight for social justice is grounded in the Judeo-Christian ethic and shaped by the visceral experience of the bottomless cruelty imposed by the institution of enslavement. The true genealogy of Black American morality is thus an issue of the stuff that's lived, felt, and molded by a spirit unique to this people's existence through American time and space. It is, as Martin Luther King, Jr., has said, "a struggle for the dignity of human personality," and nothing more. Either American rulers believe God-given rights apply to all human beings, even those with black skins, or they do not. The roots of recovery from this wretched nadir period in African American history begins at the dawn of the 20th century. W. E. B. DuBois' prophecy that "the problem of the 20th century is the problem of the color line" is an apt, compelling, and precise theme for the drama that was to take place in 20th century America. Organizations such as the Niagara Movement (1905), the National Association for the Advancement of Colored People (1909), the National Urban League (1910), and many other civil rights and Black advocacy movements which have since waxed and waned, came into being as creative responses to racial persecution, oppression, and domination. They came into being to contest the arrogance of power, that is to say racism, which means white supremacy in the American context of systematic institutional oppression. At the first Niagara Movement Convention, DuBois defined the mission, and the nature of the struggle; "We declare for ourselves full manhood rights, we accept not one dot less than our full manhood rights, and until we get these rights, we shall never cease to protest and assail the ears of America."

The first victory of the NAACP over a single aspect of white supremacy was in 1913, in a Supreme Court case known as the *"Grandfather's Clause,"* one of a myriad of racist tactics which prevented African Americans from voting. At that time, about 90% of African Americans lived in southern and border states. From the onset, the NAACP, always an integrated organization, has been in the forefront of the legal part of social struggle for African Americans. The NAACP has outlived most civil rights and Black advocacy organizations to become the most recognized champion for civil rights. Its program of (a) litigation in the American courtroom, (b) education, and (c) intelligent propaganda, has led the way. Its greatest successes have been the courtrooms from the teen years (1913 and later) to the present. A cross-section of suits and legal battles have won rights for Black people in employment, housing, and training in the professional schools in medicine, law, education, engineering, etc. This is the backdrop which led finally to *Brown v. Board of Education* in 1954. The steady "drip-drip-

drip makes a hole in the rock" program of gradualism on the part of the NAACP represents a tireless portrait in the legal fight for American democracy, and how it has been thus far won. Thurgood Marshall claimed that democracy is "Something that we do." It must be taken out of the abstract ideas and put into the trials of life as it is lived. William Hastie, the first Black person appointed to a federal judgeship and cousin of Thurgood Marshall, had this to say about the idea of democracy: "Democracy is a process and not a static condition. It is not being but becoming. It can be easily lost, and never fully won. Its essence is eternal struggle." Hastie's terse yet cogent statement on the meaning of democracy is the clearest and cleanest that I have ever read. It can scarcely be improved upon.

Thurgood Marshall

The Heart of A Lion: Charles Hamilton Houston

Charles Hamilton Houston is the unsung hero, the protagonist in this most compelling American moral, political, and social saga of the civil rights movement in 20th century America. The role of Houston represents a critical and perhaps indispensable chapter to understanding the rise of the civil rights movement in post–World War II America. His life's work is inherently bound to the "The Road to Brown." By background,

Charles Houston

Charles Hamilton Houston was the son of a lawyer and a graduate of Amherst College, which he entered at age 15 and left with a Phi Beta Kappa key. He was one of slightly more than a thousand Black officers who served in World War I, in the French theater of the war. He returned to America in 1918 determined to challenge the cavalier doctrine of white supremacy in America and its degrading "race"-based laws. As a soldier, fighting overseas to "make the world safe for democracy," he, like other Black men fighting for their country, endured many humiliating acts of racist discrimination from his fellow white American soldiers. Americans, it seemed then and now, carried the venomous disease of white supremacy wherever they appear. He was convinced that the most effective way to attack Jim Crow was through the legal system upon his return from the war. W.E.B. DuBois offered a charge for more than 200,000 Black veterans who came home from World War I: "We return from fighting. We return fighting. We won democracy abroad and by the great Jehovah we will win it at home." Accordingly, Houston earned a law degree from Harvard. While there, he was the first Black student to become editor of the Harvard Law Review. Felix Frankfurter, who would later become a Supreme Court member, described Houston as one of the most brilliant law students that he ever taught. It is poetic, and somewhat providential that one of those whom Houston later trained, his prized protégé, Thurgood Marshall, was the Chief Counsel for the NAACP who argued and won the case favoring Linda Brown and her father, a welder by trade, the Reverend Oliver Brown of Topeka, Kansas. Charles Hamilton Houston's life-long struggle amounts to a monument. Let us not forget that a "monument is that thing which causes us to remember." Thurgood Marshall has said in tribute to his mentor, "We wouldn't have gone any place if Charley hadn't laid the groundwork. I sat...waiting for my oral argument...I remember I looked around at all the lawyers present – from the NAACP from across the country. I realized there wasn't a single one of them who hadn't been touched by Charley – including me. The school case was really Charley's victory. He just never got to see it."

The downside of this otherwise glorious and life-giving victory over Jim Crow in 1954 was the fact that Charles Hamilton Houston, the lawyer-scholar-activist who labored longest to overthrow the *Plessy v. Ferguson* decision, did not live to witness his dream come true: the dismantling of legal racism. It was Houston who transformed the law school at Howard University. He organized the first class in the American Academy to specifically train lawyers in public service law. He spearheaded the accreditation of the Howard University Law School in 1935. He was not only the mentor of Thurgood Marshall but mentor to a host of other Black lawyers who stayed the course from beginning to end. It was under the tutelage of Houston that this team of lawyers accepted his command to become "social engineers." The long-term strategy designed by Houston and his brilliant team of young lawyers bordered on pure genius. He recognized that the dual educational system of the South was the achilles heel of Jim Crow. And he exploited it to break its back. By emphasizing an aggressive tactic of filing multiple suits for a truly "separate but equal" system of education, brought budgetary questions into play. The weak budgets of southern states could not possibly support two systems with equal resources. The suits insisted that Black schools receive every resource afforded to white schools; facilities, equipment, supplies, teachers, libraries, science laboratories with stock, and all other materials used by schools. This call for true equalization of pay of teachers in Black and white schools was the trump card played which would weaken the defense for segregated schools; thus, make them too expensive to maintain. The introduction of exorbitant costs to run schools was an effective example of "social engineering" for the sake of advancing democracy. His nearest contemporaries defined Houston as the most tireless and single-minded person they had ever known. He was so wholly-consumed by his work that this incomparable freedom fighter literally worked himself to death. Houston died prematurely at 56, four years before the *Brown v. Board of Education* decision was rendered.

Breaking the Silence

The Warren Court decision of 1954, now commonly called *Brown v. Board of Education*, held enormous unrecognized societal implications. It subsequently impacted on every major institution in American life. In our lifetime, the successful lawsuit by the Brown family from Topeka, Kansas, and others from across the country is a fact and concrete symbol of the courageous battle against institutional racism at the level of legal structure. As an event, *Brown v. Board* strikes a radical point of departure from the national Government's "benign neglect" of the plight of African Americans as victims of a racial caste system in American society, a caste reinforced by history, laws, religion, customs, mores, and dogmatic cultural beliefs. Historically it is the United States Government itself that is the major culprit in this flagrant miscarriage of justice against Black Americans. The government over many years consistently refused to do

(l. to r. seated) Felix Frankfurter, Hugo L. Black, Earl Warren, Stanley F. Reed, William O. Douglas. (l. to r. standing) Tom C. Clark, Robert H. Jackson, Harold H. Burton, Sherman Minton

what it was mandated to do since the Civil War amendments, and that is to protect the rights of all of its citizens as individuals from the harm of their more aggressive brothers. This governmental malfeasance occurred with the apparent consent of the American people by their silence, and thus violated their own creed that "all men are endowed by their Creator with certain inalienable rights." The 14th Amendment says that an individual is not a "race," but Americans have been smothered by indoctrination that "race" is real irrespective of individuality when it comes to Black folks. The objectification of Black people by whiteness is at the core of "race" as a function of power over Black people. "Being white" argued James Baldwin, "is not a color. It is a state of mind. It's even a moral choice."

The *Brown v. Board of Education* decision compares in historical importance to the *Dred Scott* decision of 1857 as well as the aforementioned *Plessy v. Ferguson* decision. These two previous decisions represent the most significant antidemocratic interpretations of the Constitution in the 19th century with  "race" at its core. Together, they give us the most compelling examples of the legal suppression of Black human rights before the turn of the century.

Dred Scott

The 1954 Decision against school segregation reversed the lock-step trend of the executive, legislative, and judiciary branches of the U.S. Government's overt complicity in nullifying the previously hard-won constitutional rights of African Americans. These aforementioned rights were added to the Constitution between 1865 and 1870. There were, also, two strong enabling civil rights bills passed in 1866 and 1875. The *Brown* decision signaled the end of the unchallenged domination of racist powerbrokers who had been the yoke around national domestic policy regarding "race" relations since the overthrow of Reconstruction, up until the maturation and power of the civil rights movement rose to challenge them. The presidential election of Rutherford B. Hayes of Ohio over Samuel Tilden of New York in 1876 signalled the end of the tenuous protection of the constitutional rights of Black Americans. Tilden, the winner of the popular vote, lost the presidency through the electoral college after a promise by Hayes to withdraw the last of the Union troops from the South. (This historic fact is not totally unrelated to the George W. Bush non-election by popular vote in 2000. In both cases unabashed corruption prevailed.) The usurpation of African American legal rights by established authority has no doubt been the republic's greatest vice. The U.S. Government itself represents historically a gross and undeniable violation of what we now know as "The Universal Declaration of Human Rights" by the U.N. The equal protection clause in the 14th Amendment of the Constitution of the United States was studiously ignored over the many decades. If we don't know this about America, then we don't know America.

Nearly 59 years of governmental silence would reign before African Americans would again emerge as a dominant editorial force in American political life. During all of these officially silent years, Blacks were persistently waging a gallant, but unrecognized struggle against the stench of widespread racial oppression and governmental failure to regard the Black right to democracy. Here and there, were some half-hearted restoration of constitutional rights, but it took a World War to prompt the government to change its patented racial policies. Through Black struggle, the right to citizenship has been uncertainly, and incrementally won. The style, posture, and spirit of American political leadership was forced by a new set of postwar conditions to acknowledge the existence of Black people in a way that it had not been accustomed to doing, which thereby opened a vent for creative tensions to be released anew.

The period following the second World War would thus become the fabric upon which the continuing struggle for Black rights would be woven. And the *Brown* decision became the unanticipated catalyst, the ace in the hole, for new flights of the human spirit, new schools of thought, and new fights for new freedoms for Blacks, and by extension, the vast numbers of white citizens who were then largely disinterested bystanders, seemingly unaware of the unfinished work in American democracy and its shortcomings, regarding their own rights as American citizens. "There arose a generation, who know not Joseph"; they, the whites, knew not the distance between professed ideals and the reality of pragmatic power.

Let us consider for a moment the immediate historical setting and the underbelly of the Court ruling that would signal a new age of protest and possibilities for Black people. The time was nearly nine years after World War II, two years after a nagging recession (the 1952 Eisenhower depression for Blacks), one year after the end of the so-called Korean Conflict. It was a time of the excesses: a Wisconsin Senator, Joseph McCarthy, unleashed the terrifying Communist witch hunt, putting fear in the hearts of many Americans and destroying the good reputations of many men and women unfairly accused of being Communist agents. On the other hand, ironically enough, it was also a time when the salable image of America was that of a self-assured, proud, smug, and innocent acting middle-class sleeping beauty. America, then, was the Affluent Society that John Kenneth Gilbraith mused about. America, then, was a collection of status seekers that Vance Packard described in his trilogy of books about consumerism and the pleasure principle, chiding his fellow Americans. America was the "White Man," that wouldn't "listen" to the warnings of novelist Richard Wright.

On the international front, America was evidencing itself as the unchallenged policeman of the "free world's" interests, and the fiercest enemy of the Communist Worldwide Menace. In that age of the Cold War between America, the rest of the west, and the Soviet Union, an intense struggle for the hearts and minds of men who were neither Communist, capitalist, nor Christian, dominated much of the geopolitics of the world. The unruffled and smiling face of America presented an even surface to much of the world, while self-deceivingly covering the volcanic disruptions which were her uneven bottom. This was thus the strangest irony, the double-edged sword; Sleeping Beauty and Frankenstein wedded together. Unsuspectingly, this uneven bottom would soon expose the United States as a society that was one of the most shamelessly hypocritical and racist in the world. At this point in history, with the demise of Nazi Germany, the fact of America's overt racism could be matched only by the Republic of South Africa's peculiar brand of fascism: its introduction of Apartheid in 1948. On the face of things, the might of white was right and seemed undisturbed, confidently invincible. Always, there are at least two things that can be true. It was time for Langston Hughes' "Dream," which had been "deferred," to "explode."

A. Phillip Randolph: A Seed of the New Militancy

Historians can cite only a few instances of relatively unobscure and positive action by federal authority on behalf of the God-given rights of Blacks prior to *Brown v. Board*. The two most significant were executive orders by Presidents Franklin Delano Roosevelt and Harry S. Truman. Roosevelt issued executive order 8802, authorizing the Fair Employment Practice

A. Phillip Randolph

Commission, which challenged unfair discrimination against Blacks in the war industries in 1941. It took A. Phillip Randolph, the great labor leader and his status as a Black leader (and "the most dangerous Negro in America" according to an editorial in the New York Times in 1935), to force the issue with FDR over jobs for "Negroes" in the rapidly emerging war industries. Randolph threatened a march on Washington that would bring 10,000 strong to the nation's capital. This was to be an all-Black march. The progressive whites of that day seemed to understand that such an act was absolutely necessary. The "All Black" march was a very intelligent tactic as a part of an overall strategy. Randolph called for this tactic in order for "Negroes to build confidence in one another." This had nothing whatsoever to do with keeping freedom-loving white people out of the movement. Frederick Douglass said it best: "The man struck, is the man to cry out. He who has endured the cruel pangs of slavery is one man to advocate liberty." Randolph applied a "Black power" tactic, long before that unsettling and controversial slogan came to American consciousness. FDR acquiesced and issued the Fair Employment Practices Commission edict, and the march was called off.

Next, Harry Truman issued executive order 9981, reluctantly desegregating the Armed Forces in 1948. Once again, this was as a result of a threatened March by Randolph and his legions. As concessions, they were made grudgingly, when we recall that it was only through the daring and uncompromising militancy of this creative labor leader of the Brotherhood of Sleeping Car Porters, that these concessions were made. It took the twice-threatened all Black march on Washington claiming 10,000 strong, before two presidents, out of fear of international embarrassment, if not domestic chaos, would make these concessions.

A. Phillip Randolph's Grand March on Washington "for jobs and freedom" finally came true 23 years later on August 28, 1963, where young Martin Luther King would articulate his historic and celebrated "I Have a Dream" speech before a fully integrated crowd of 300,000 or more people in front of the Lincoln Memorial, "in whose symbolic shadow we stand." With the aid of television, America marveled at the discipline, dignity, and eloquence of this march, the largest in history up to that point in time, a spirit unprecedented until this time. Every ethnic group was represented, every marginalized group with an axe to grind was there, including Gays and Lesbians, one of whom was the major organizer of this show of democracy and the principle of inclusion. This march presaged what we now call multiculturalism, "people of color," multiracialism, etc. This march became the model for all future mass demonstrations in our nation's capital. The mantra of the man who conceived of this great idea, A. Phillip Randolph, was organization and power. He was strongly convinced that "organization is the fruit and flower of power." He once declared, "at the banquet table of nature, there are no free lunches. If you can't take anything, you won't get anything; if you can't hold anything, you won't keep anything, and you can't get anything without organization!"

By an ironic twist of fate, 1954 became a pivotal year in Black – as well as wider – American history. That decision, handed down by the High Court, marks an event that simultaneously raised new political challenges for others as well as new directions for Black struggle. It is worthy to note that the Supreme Court Decision was inspired by neither Christian love nor humane values, but by unavoidable political reality. This is so because the Supreme Court is in part a political institution. Yet the myth prevails that the High Court is really above society, cloistered in a cloud of pious objectivity, above the influence of political weight and complexity of the world. Witness appointments to the Supreme Court according to political ideology. What does this mean? Like all good and sensible politicians, the Court made a practical (not a moral) choice that would serve political ends. To repeat, the *Brown* decision was thus a political decision, not one that can be measured by simple justice grounded in morality. Again, the great old sage and abolitionist leader, Frederick Douglass, has left us an apt description of this kind of political behavior: "They do wrong from choice and right from necessity."

Frederick Douglass

Unsung Champions at Home and Abroad

Let us consider the context of the times from both a domestic and foreign relations perspective. More often than not, these two things mean one thing. That is to say, foreign and domestic policies are but the two sides of the same horse. A good while before the *Brown* decision, the intelligence agencies of the United States, of which we have learned so very much about lately, knew earlier than the common citizen that a storm was brewing at home and abroad. The progressive leadership within the Black population in the U.S. had matured to the point of recognizing that Black people would be a factor in the Cold War. They discovered that they were "a key people in a key country." They knew, and knew for a very long time, that the American government's image was vulnerable as the professed bearer and protector of human freedoms the world over when in fact, Black people were blatantly denied simple justice here in the "land of the free." American political leadership, at bottom, was (and remains) hypocritical. To progressive Black leaders and progressive whites as well, the condition of Black people was overwhelming proof of that fact. Progressive leadership among Blacks made every effort to exploit and expose America as the racist monster that it was. Three brief and significant examples are in order.

First, in 1948 William L. Patterson, a distinguished African American lawyer from New York, attempted to submit to the U.N. his description of home-grown atrocities committed against Black people. (For instance, 1952 was the first year of the 20th century in which a Black human being was not publicly murdered by lynching. No single person was ever prosecuted for such

William Patterson

deeds. To this day, there is no federal law against lynching. Why?) His tract was entitled, "We Charge Genocide." Patterson charged the U.S. with violation of Black human rights under the U.N. Universal Declaration of Human Rights, before his voice was summarily suppressed. It should be noted that in 1947 the NAACP itself attempted to bring America before the bar of world opinion with a petition protesting America's ill treatment of its Black citizens. W. E. B. DuBois was the petition's principal author. DuBois claimed "it was not the Soviet Union that threatened the United States and its beloved democracy, but Mississippi's leaders." This effort was also suppressed by the misuse of American power; that is, the U.S. delegation to the U.N. refused to introduce the petitions to the General Assembly.

Secondly, there is Paul Robeson, the great scholar and the most famous of all American faces around the world. He was also one of the most beloved public figures in the world as an athlete, scholar, concert artist, actor, lawyer, linguist, and political activist. Here was a Black man, who despite his fame and material success, remained loyal to his convictions and was passionately devoted to the freedom of his people and

Paul Robeson

the democratic principles for which they for so long struggled. Moreover, he spoke in more than a dozen nations of the world for Black freedom and the rights of the working class the world over. He was known by the great masses of people throughout Europe, especially the socialist world. When he returned to this country after living 12 years of self-imposed exile in Europe (1932-1944), he was a marked man. He was "Red and Black," the very worst possible thing to be. In 1949, the so-called Peekskill Riot in outstate New York occurred. Robeson was violently hounded from the stage by police and townspeople to keep thousands of willing listeners from hearing him sing and speak. So much for free speech. This happened despite his earlier contribution to American propaganda, with the making of *The Ballad of the Americans*, a recording sent around the world to ramp up the American image as the land of the free. His case is a classic example of a basic civil rights violation, the sacred right of an individual to dissent. Robeson was a relentless enemy of American injustice to Blacks and working class people. He was the American answer to Alexander Solzhenitsyn, the much heralded dissenting writer from the Soviet Union in the 1980s. Both of these gifted artists were used as tools of propaganda in the Cold War by the respective leaders of their countries – the Iron Curtain versus the Cotton Curtain. For his uncompromising stance against American injustice, Robeson's passport was taken so he could not work in this country nor any place else. His work as an artist was silenced on every front; for eight years, one could not go to a Robeson concert, nor see a Robeson movie, nor buy a Robeson recording. For eight years Paul Robeson's name could not be printed in a mainstream American newspaper. His civil rights were cancelled and he was investigated by the House Unamerican Activities Committee (HUAC), a motley collective of antidemocratic, Jefferson-Davis–Black-hating white supremacists and their allies, northern conservative highbrow racists; among them was a young ambitious congressman from California, Richard Milhous Nixon. The House Unamerican Activities Committee was a contradiction in terms. Those who presumed themselves to be the guardians of American ideals, were also its most conspicuous enemies. An echo from Frederick Douglass: "If the gentlemen are sincere, they are insensible. If they are sensible, they are insincere." The major source of the power of this committee came from seniority gained by denying one-third of the

(Black) population of the South to vote. In short, Robeson was politically assassinated. Support from a broad cross-section of the people of Western Europe was in large part responsible for the U.S. State Department lifting the travel ban on Robeson in 1958, after nearly a decade of silencing his voice. The tragedy of Robeson presages the persecution of Muhammad Ali, caused by his refusal to submit to military draft and to fight for a country in which he could not enjoy the simple act of having lunch at a downtown counter because of Jim Crow laws and customs in his hometown. Robeson was the epitome of courage, strength, integrity, and respect for the peoplehood of all. He once asserted that "in my music, in my art, in my scholarship, in my athletic achievements, I am always first and foremost an African."

Thirdly, the redoubtable scholar, W. E. B. DuBois, another progressive patriot for Black freedom, was similarly labeled and, like Robeson, restricted by the State Department for his prodemocracy activities; he was eventually arrested as a foreign agent (read communist). (Over the years the role of such men and women in the making of democracy, including Mary

W.E.B. Dubois

Church Terrell and Ida B. Wells, Pauli Murray, and latter-day women radicals such as Ella Baker, Ruby Doris Robinson, Diane Nash, Annie Devine, Victoria Gray, Gloria Richardson, and Fannie Lou Hamer, who dissented by criticizing the American government, is not generally appreciated. Most of them ranked high at one time or another on FBI and CIA lists – as was the NAACP and the Black press – as subversives, dangerous to domestic tranquility. Who can forget Fannie Lou Hamer's soul-stirring and eloquent statement "I question America," at the Democratic Convention in 1964.) In typical, militant DuBois fashion, DuBois thumbed his nose at the American power structure by renouncing his American citizenship in 1961 to become a citizen of an African nation (Ghana) and insisted that his remains be interred on African soil beside a Christenborg, a slave dungeon. He joined the Communist Party before the eyes of the world – in Moscow in 1962 – at the age of 94. DuBois, forever, principled, honest, fearless, and idealistic, DuBois died on August 27, 1963, the eve of the great March on Washington, at the age of 95.

In the international arena, due to the aftermath of World War II, the world was being reorganized in geopolitical terms. The United Nations was established in San Francisco in 1945. This institution gave a breath of fresh air to "the unwashed masses of the earth." By 1954, U.N. Ambassador Adlai Stevenson declared "the revolution of rising expectations" to be clearly a force to be reckoned with. This "revolution" entailed the decolonization of Asia, Africa, and the islands of the sea. Liberating nationalist movements reacting to centuries of Western exploitation via imperialism, colonialism, and racism had exploded. That is to say, European and American economic exploitation, political dominance, cultural suppression, and racial arrogance, was being challenged everywhere. The western world, which claimed to be the undisputed civilizers and masters of the modern world, found itself between the jaws of a vice. That vice was the international communist movement (outside) and the creative and powerful movement for democracy inside the belly of America – i.e. the civil rights movement. "The Wretched of the Earth" said "No!" in the words of Franz Fanon, to the continued hegemony of white supremacy on the world stage. The concept of "the white man's burden" was on its last legs. The British Empire, so vast it was said that the sun would never set on it, had crumbled so that now the sun couldn't find the British Empire. Let us revisit the anti-imperialist polemics of Mark Twain, which stirs our recall of those horrific times:

> *In many countries we have chained the savage and starved him to death...in many countries. We burned the savage at the stake...We have hunted the savage and his little children and their mother with dogs and guns...in many countries we have taken the savage's land from him, and made him our slave, and lashed him every day and broken his pride and made death his only friend, and over worked him till dropped in his tracks... And, there are many humorous things in this world, among them the white man's notion that he is less savage than other savages.*

A largely nonwhite world was now snatching its humanity out of the fiery flames of their deformed and defamed histories, reclaiming and reconstructing their dignity as fully fleshed human beings. By 1954 the independence of India, Indonesia, and Egypt were geopolitical facts. The political independence of many African states was inevitable a few years hence. It is not without significance that the Bandung Conference was held in 1954. The Bandung Conference (Indonesia) was a meeting of the nonaligned colored peoples of the world. The western man was barred from this conference. The Soviet Union – purely by accident of history a power whose hands remained uncontaminated as a major oppressor of the colored mass of humanity outside its sphere of influence – gleefully waited in the wings for political advantage in the Cold War with the hated West. A liberated Chinese mainland gloated. The explosion of African independence movements was waiting in the wings: Ghana – the former British colony named the Gold Coast – would rise as the first independent African state, three years later, in 1957. American foreign policy, with its haughty disrespect for the colored peoples of the world, became its Achilles heel. By 1961, "The Year of Africa," nearly a dozen new states claimed their independence. These powerful creative forces on the world stage had both inspired and energized "the movement" within the borders of the United States – that is to say, the civil rights movement. In a recent work, <u>Silent</u>

Covenants, Derrick Bell boldly titles one of the chapters "Brown as an Anticommunist Decision." Need I say more.

This, then, is a capsule impression of the domestic and international political climate at roughly the time that the Supreme Court took its official antiracist stand. If America were to maintain its impressive, but transparent image as the great bastion of human freedom, it was absolutely necessary to move with the winds of change that were taking place among most of the people who inhabit this earth. These people, the third world, coincidentally, were created by the same forces in the modern world that had created the "American Negro" over the last 500 years. Imperialism and colonialism are inherently akin to racism, slavery, and capitalism; they are cut from the same cloth. They could be cut with the same blade.

It has been sometimes noted by critical minds that the Black population in the United States has represented a glaringly contradictory reality throughout its history. This nation state was born in contradiction: DuBois, "Home of the free and the land of the slave"; a house of refuge and a house of bondage.

These two indisputable historical truths are at the heart of contemporary "race" problems. The fact that two things can be true seems never to occur to most Americans. On the one hand, Black people are and have historically been an asset to America; as a super-exploited cheap source of labor and the most persistent unwitting patriotic soldiers in every official American war, not to mention the Black people's immense contribution in continuously shaping what we are pleased to call American culture yesterday and today. On the other hand, Black people can be viewed as a liability; as the most "man despised and God possessed" people in the American republic, they are an aggrieved class of Americans; thus, they represent the greatest natural threat for changing the social order. Their revolutionary potential is obvious to whoever may be America's enemy at the time. The constant surveillance of Black people has not changed since the days of their enslavement. They are over-scrutinized, be it on a plantation or in an urban ghetto. Clearly, the underlying meaning of the *Brown* decision was keenly related to the transparently twin realities of American domestic and foreign relations. What better way to show the world, and progressive forces at home, that America was really sincere in its celebrated claim that "all men are endowed with certain inalienable rights." So, then, Black people once again were used as an asset by the American power structure for the sake of devising a new international strategy and image-change as a nation which respected the rights of all people, including, "the real people of color," African people, who remain in, but not of America. What better way to convince the world that America had mended her ways and was now a humane nation because it did not suppress nor persecute any segment of its population; it did not despise its dispossessed or restrict freedom because of cultural differences. So the stage was set by the Supreme Court when it ran the first leg of new governmental strategies by spawning the American image as a nonracist, culturally pluralistic, and liberal political democracy. In effect, the *Brown* decision was a huge public relations gimmick for international consumption. At home, things were a bit more ambiguous on the part of this triangle of Black people, their white allies, and their relentless racist enemies. 400 years of Black distrust is a difficult habit to break, despite some sense of relief by the Court which gave Black people a bit of new social space. An immediate shift from suspicion to trustfulness would be a very stunning trick to pull off, in the light of deep-seated racial attitudes based on what Thomas Jefferson called "ten thousand recollections, by Blacks, of injuries they have sustained...." This new playing field would prove a challenge to the racist power structure and some in the liberal camp as well.

The Politics of the Supreme Court

The Supreme Court Decision must be seen in the light of a set of political and social facts. Once again: the *Brown* decision was a political decision. Why was not such a decision rendered in 1944? or 1934? And why in the year of our Lord, 1954? Was not segregation just as real? Just as evil? Was not the letter and spirit of the Constitution violated before 1954? It has ever been thus, concerning the history of Black people in U.S. To this day, no freedoms have been won by Black Americans because of human generosity, or by action deriving from Judeo-Christian beliefs (save by the public discourse, ingeniously applied by Martin Luther King, Jr.), or a common sense expression of fair play. Black victories over parts of this encyclopedic monster called racism always result from a convergence of political necessity forced on the system. Black people often create the necessity. The commanding words of Frederick Douglass should be written in the sky for all of the world's oppressed: "If there is no struggle, there is no progress."

Of the three branches of federal authority, the Supreme Court has always been best suited to facilitate the progress or reversal of social change. It is far less cumbersome for the nine-man Court (which now includes women) to cultivate a new political climate than an often stormily divisive and emotionally charged legislature. Then too, the Court is far more able (because of its relative remoteness from public scrutiny) than a morally coward president or a game-playing amoral Congress to render a ground-breaking political decision. In relation to Black people, the history of the Supreme Court is a history of political decisions, reflecting the climate of the times. The obvious examples have already been alluded to: *Scott v. Sandford*, better known as the *Dred Scott* decision of 1857, in which Chief Justice Roger B.

Taney, articulating that "For nigh two centuries these persons (Blacks) have been viewed as beings of an inferior order, so far inferior that they had no rights that Whites were bound to respect," clearly supported the institutions of Black enslavement. He further stated that, "[Blacks] are not included, and were not included, under the word 'citizens' in the Constitution." This meant that Black people north, as well as south, could not be citizens of the United

Roger B. Taney

States, which is to say, they did not officially possess a nationality. Black people were not a part of the American polity. It is worthwhile to note that the fundamental and distinctive nationality of Black Americans comes not from a piece of paper but from the unique history of an enslaved population. Nationalities are derived from two sources in life: History and politics. The nationality of Black folk is created by a history of authentically lived, felt, and known experiences. Nationality deriving from the 14th Amendment is political, and therefore, for the most part, artificial for Black folk. The fact that Taney and several others on the bench at that time were or had been slaveholders was the clearest example of highbrow immorality; the repeal of Black Civil Rights Acts (1866–1875) by 1883; and the *Plessy v. Ferguson* decision of 1896; the *Bakke* decision of 1978; the *Weber* decision, etc.

These latter-day 20th century decisions initiated the assault against the hard won and recently sanctioned affirmative action programs, very much in step with the political climate of the times in reaction to the gains won by the morally outraged civil rights movement. Today, save for mostly middle class white women, affirmative action is dead in the water. Black Americans, the bearers of the cross for affirmative action, remain the Christ-like figure; they are the face of affirmative action, though not the major beneficiaries. What all of these decisions add up to are political acts which respond to political reality which tempers a national consensus. Political climate and political activity will, in turn, legitimate or repudiate the validity of the decision. Baring the *Dred Scott* decision of 1857, which was nullified by passage of the 14th Amendment in 1868, Supreme Court decisions have been a key part of social change, regressive or progressive. Hence, *Plessy v. Ferguson* was in effect overturned by the *Brown v. Board of Education* decision, and the *Bakke v. University of California* decision modified the impact of affirmative action. The backlash, unleashed by Republican presidential candidate Barry Goldwater in 1964, set the stage for reactionary political movement towards the Black-led civil rights struggle in America. Goldwater, who renounced his Judaism for whiteness, is the radical reference point for the present Republican Party. In the shrillest of voices, he announced that, "Moderation in pursuit of justice is no virtue. Extremism in defense of liberty is no vice," to which he received thunderous applause along with inspiring an intimidating political environment. This stance is what drew the white supremacist Strom Thurmond to the Republican Party. In short, the past three decades or so add up to an ideological and antithetical reaction to the previous decades of civil rights gains. The party of Lincoln and of the Emancipation Proclamation has thus been hijacked by a not-too-disguised coalition of the big business class and the bearers of anti-Black racism. The same racist bullies who once obstructed decent sensibilities among some Democrats are now Republicans. Richard Nixon's "southern strategy" consummated the political takeover of the white South.

Let's recall in earnest that the struggle to pressure the U.S. Government to officially abolish the racist systems of education in America was a long and arduous one, beginning well before World War II. The NAACP, the legal arm of the civil rights movement and a sterling example of consistency and responsibility, had been filing suits challenging Jim Crow education since the late 1920s. On a case-by-case basis, the NAACP confronted the evils of racial discrimination in almost every border and southern state. It first succeeded in winning cases that allowed Blacks to enter the graduate and professional schools in border states such as Oklahoma, Arkansas, Missouri, and Maryland. By the late 1950s, Blacks had won the right to gain graduate training in all of these states. With this kind of persistence, it was only a matter of time before Black relentless struggle, coupled with world political and economic realities, would dictate political necessity on the part of the principalities and powers of America. The once nascent civil rights movement and the national government, because of new dynamics in the world of power politics, found themselves moving in the same political direction. This made for either a shotgun marriage or Caesarean operation. Will Rogers said it best: "All is fair in love and war, and in politics, it's even fairer." The pragmatic union between the extra-legal popular social movement for "Negro civil rights" and legitimate authority was effected, and this tactical alliance ushered in a new age of government responsibility to social justice. Ralph Ellison's <u>Invisible Man</u>, at long last, had arisen from the underground.

The Movement: No Longer Invisible

The pace of social change quickened at break-neck speed between 1954 and 1964. Like a whirlwind on the heels of *Brown v. Board of Education* came the Interstate Commerce Commission ruling in early 1955. The ICC issued a regulation giving all Americans the right to ride public conveyance from state to state, irrespective of local custom – that is, the rules of southern law. The law of the land had nudged another branch of government to act. Ancillary to this discussion were two critical events which heightened Black, as well as white, American consciousness. First, the unspeakable murder of 14-year-old Emmett Till in Money, Mississippi, in August 1955. It was this powerfully tragic event which made the entire world conscious about what was really going on in America. Secondly, just a few months later, on December 1, 1955, with the heroic stance against the patented humiliation of segregation by that noble and courageous seamstress, Rosa Parks, the Montgomery Bus Boycott was all but endorsed by the will of the people. The bus boycott evolved into a powerful local organization called the Montgomery Improvement Association. The initiator and titular head of the movement was E. D. Nixon, leader of the NAACP. Mrs. Parks was his secretary; Mr. Nixon was a member of the union founded by A. Phillip Randolph, the Brotherhood of Sleeping Car Porters. The movement was launched almost unanimously by 50,000 Black citizens of Montgomery, Alabama. After 381 days the boycott reached successful conclusion, thereby setting a creative example of how political democracy,

E.D. Nixon

when given a chance, really works. It is always the voluntary segment of society which calls democracy from theory into play. The quietly evolving practice of participatory democracy was given new flights of inspiration by this successful movement for social change by a single creative Black community. The event was to forever change the character and consciousness of Black and white America. The success of the Montgomery Bus Boycott went way beyond Montgomery. It was another one of those great rare moments when idea and experience united and spread like the gospel. It was, in effect, a school of public instruction in community-organization fortitude for the entire nation. Here is one of the best examples of Margaret Mead's assertion that "a small group of thoughtful, committed people can change the world. Indeed, that is the only thing that ever has." This was the first significant example in postwar America of the philosophy of massive passive-nonviolent resistance in American history. Henry David Thoreau's individual practice of civil disobedience was elevated to a mass scale of social power, "of power to the people." The boycott was a concrete expression of the spirit informed by the practical obsession of the Supreme Court.

This movement, unpredictably, produced something else – a very young, little known, well-trained and educated Baptist minister by the name of Martin Luther King, Jr. He, by time and circumstance and with the ingenuity of E. D. Nixon, became the voice of this movement and led this historic campaign with a compelling moral declaration to a church overcrowded with conservative Black and brave Christians, the likes of which the American Republic had never seen. What Martin Luther King called "this marvelous new militancy on the part of the Negro," was the radical element of the Christian creed, introduced as an unprecedented act in 20th century social movement. He went on to say, "We are not wrong in what we are doing. If we are wrong, then the Declaration of Independence is wrong; if we are wrong, the Constitution of the United States is wrong; if we are wrong, the Bill of Rights is wrong; if we are wrong, the Supreme

Court is wrong; if we are wrong, God almighty is wrong." This became the moral high ground which sustained the struggle for democracy for more than a decade.

The idea of social action, nonviolent and direct, served to capture the imagination of much of nation: The Little Rock Nine at Central High School in Little Rock, Arkansas, was the first major test in attempting the desegregation of public schools in 1957. Under the able mentorship of Daisy Bates, a local NAACP teacher, nine brave students, confronted by mobs before the eyes of the world, forced the hand of the U.S. Government. A middle-of-the-road

Daisy Bates

president, Dwight Eisenhower, was forced by necessity to do something which no President had done since the Reconstruction era. Eisenhower used federal troops to enforce the law of the land against a renegade South – which, after all, did lose the Civil War. Federal troops were called in to enforce the law, which can only be exercised by executive authority. The Constitution gives the President the powers to execute the law. This fact seems to escape most, even informed, Americans – and that is that legislation is not needed to do what the Constitution already assures by executive authority. So then, it was executive authority that was needed to protect the rights of Black people all the while, if they are indeed citizens.

Movements always produce unexpected twists and turns. One such surprise was a genius of the trumpet, who had been used for years as a Goodwill ambassador to bolster the American image abroad. Louis Armstrong, whose artistic gifts were long overshadowed by being falsely labeled an

Elizabeth Eckford - Little Rock. Arkansas

"Uncle Tom" by unthinking segments of the Black community, became an unlikely hero because he stunned the U.S. power structure by refusing to go to Europe as a State Department sponsored Goodwill ambassador. His refusal was in reaction to the Little Rock crisis and the bitterness that it caused. "These cats would persecute Jesus if he were here," was Satchmo's indictment of the leadership of the Governor of Arkansas, Orville Faubus. No President since Ulysses S. Grant had exercised in a meaningful way the power of the institution of the presidency, and that was to execute the law to protect the rights of Black people. President after president seemed to have little trouble in exercising power to spread "democracy" abroad; Panama, Cuba, Grenada, Haiti, Iraq, ad nauseam, but rarely in the interest of making democracy work for Black people and the indigenous (American Indian) populations at home.

In the field of direct action, a radical dimension was added with student pickets and sit-ins and freedom rides. The idealistic Black students from historically Black colleges and universities of the early 1960s engaged in eyeball-to-eyeball confrontation with discrimination, and telescoped time. They achieved in a relatively brief period of time what dozens of lawsuits could not have done in a long stretch of years. In terms of the growth of American democracy, the Black sons and daughters, grandsons and granddaughters of sharecroppers, tenant farmers, and bondsmen in the American South, are the first American students to become truly politicized by actual experience in the struggle for social justice. The first to become engaged in non-campus centered *real politik*. They inspired white students at the elite schools in the North to abandon longstanding outbursts of panty raids, riotous spring breaks, goldfish swallowing, beer busts, crowding in telephone booths, and mud slides, to become engaged in meaningful protest and social action. A new idealism emerged, the like of which had not been seen since the days of the abolitionist movement against the institution of slavery, the grandfather of segregation. Beginning with four freshman from historically Black North Carolina A&T College, in Greensboro, North Carolina, on February 1, 1960, thousands of Black students would rapidly join the four freshmen from over 50 Black colleges and universities in protest throughout that spring season. Over two thousand went to jail for their sacrificial acts; sit-ins, read-ins, wade-ins and pray-ins. By May of 1960, for all intents and purposes, the South had been desegregated by Black students. From these protests, the first politicized student organization emerged: the Student Nonviolent Coordinating Committee, or "Snick," as it became commonly known. It was the first organization of its kind from American college campuses. The southern Negro Youth Congress of the 1920s, noble though that cause was, never really got off the ground.

During the early rise of the movement for democracy, and in rapid succession, two minor civil rights bills were passed in 1957 and 1960. Oddly enough, these bills were steered through Congress by Lyndon Baines Johnson, a senator and majority whip from Texas, who had been a longtime enemy to

Black people as a staunch segregationist of the solid South. Politics at its best is the art of the possible, and Lyndon B. Johnson was a master of this art. When this southern former segregationist died, he was hailed by many Black spokespersons as the president who had done most in the cause of human and civil rights for Blacks; beyond Lincoln and Kennedy. This is all despite the fact that Johnson, under the able tutelage of his mentor and segregationist Sam Rayburn, had opposed nearly every piece of civil rights legislation for two decades prior to 1957. He tested the winds of change and followed accordingly. Politics, indeed, makes strange bedfellows.

By the 1960s, the climate for social change that had been tactfully engendered by the Supreme Court ruling pervaded the entire social climate of America. First in the South, then the North, the Civil Rights Acts of 1964-65 and 1968 were the legislative companions to the ruling by the Earl Warren court. A host of regulations by bureaucratic agencies and presidential behavior affirmed the principle of equal justice for all before the reactionary Nixon election of 1968 united Black and white together in singing "We Shall Overcome."

Chief Justice Earl Warren

The Supreme Court Decision of 1954, without question, made a major contribution to the spirit of the times. But as always in the realm of political reality, in a political democracy it is the people, as forestated, the voluntary segment of society, which creates meaningful social change. No government ever has and never will initiate progressive social change. Governments respond to movements for social change. And change we have. Freedom summer of 1964 and the heroic assault on racism in the state of Mississippi was to change national politics. This was a time in which the Mississippi Freedom Democratic Party was founded. People such as Fannie Lou Hamer, Bob Moses, and Lawrence Goyet were leaders of the most significant event in 20th century electoral politics in America. The Mississippi challenge was to force the Democratic Party to open its doors to all of its constituency – African Americans, women, indigenous peoples, Mexicans, and other ethnic minorities. In 1964 the Democratic Party, north and south, was in effect a collection of all-white male clubs. It was the uncompromising struggle of the Mississippi Freedom Democratic Party which made the Democrats a true national political party by 1968. In order to keep up appearances, the Republican Party had to open its doors to their left-outs by 1972. Nearly every new value that we now possess regarding war and peace, poverty, racism and antiracism, ecology, crime, student rights, sexism, or sexual orientation, treatment of minorities, treatment of the physically handicapped, and the rights of children and the elderly, are derived from the spirit of those times. The Supreme Court – the last stop on the line of the American system of justice – made a political decision which facilitated political action, which in turn has brought America to the crossroads with itself. The creative connections with the foregoing influences are perhaps the African American's greatest contribution to the American style of political democracy. And at the same time, it is the Black population that is least likely to reap a real harvest from social progress. That has been the dilemma for Black America: it creates avenues for change, in the way that it creates

Fannie Lou Hamer

original music. Progress for Black Americans meant, and still means, progress for everyone. The Creator patently reaps fewest rewards, ending up in an alley of stagnation.

All Deliberate Speed

Before the ink was dry on the original decision of 1954, a second decision was handed down in 1955. Of the voluminous words that were spoken and written by the Court in 1955, the most striking three to remember were: "All deliberate speed." From this it is obvious that the Court had second thoughts about what it had done. So then, to complete the whole meaning of the two *Brown v. Board* decisions it became necessary to qualify the meaning of the first. All of the wording about the unspeakable damage that segregation was doing to the mind, hearts, and spirits of vulnerable Black children aside, the Court saw the need to tweak the previous edict. "All deliberate speed" was certainly a powerful caveat to a hopeful Black community that would be cause for some uneasiness. The same words, on the other hand were conversely reassuring to the forces of Jim Crow, the system of longtime oppression. The second decision was, in effect, a sheltered signal to the leadership of the white South that it need

Ruby Bridges

not be too alarmed, by implying that the dismantling of the segregated institutions was a while away. "All deliberate speed" thus was up in the air for interpretation, and the active meaning of the interpretation was immediately seized by the most active agents which sought to preserve segregation and the long-held idea and practice of white supremacy.

"All deliberate speed" was inherently suggestive of making all deliberate speed become, in fact, all deliberate delay. Hence the demise of segregation won't be tomorrow, and may very well be never. So the enemies of social and racial progress ingeniously developed a number of dilatory tactics to hold off, if not outright defeat, the intent of the letter and spirit of the original *Brown v. Board* decision of 1954. Most southern political leaders adopted the stance of massive resistance to integration in any form. The White Citizen's Council, an aggregate of leading southern businessmen, after an inexplicable period of quiet delay, rapidly organized to contest the decision and its threat to "our way of life." The South's most conspicuous political leaders, such as Strom Thurmond, James Eastland, John Stennis, and Richard Russell, encouraged their constituencies to fight "the tyranny of federal power." Of these, one of the most militant exponents of resistance to democratic progress was Strom Thurmond, long known since the 1948 Democratic Convention, when he and his "Dixiecrat" followers bolted the

Strom Thurmond

party in reaction to Minnesota Senator Hubert Humphrey's eloquent demand for the inclusion of a rather mild civil rights plank in the democratic platform. Of all the rabid racists of that day, Thurmond commanded the most attention as a champion of white supremacy. This is the same Strom Thurmond from South Carolina who lived to be 100 years old, and who served longer (roughly a half century) than any person in the history of the U.S. Senate. Thus, the same Strom Thurmond who stood on the floor of the Congress for 24 hours and 8 minutes, filibustering against the civil rights bill of 1957, is the same Strom Thurmond who fathered a Black child by a 16-year-old girl while preaching and teaching a doctrine of racial separation. Segregationist by day, cunningly and incessantly (in the flesh) integrationist by night. This was the pattern of scores of southern white men since antebellum days. This man was the epitome of the reprobates who represented the white South: half-literate, hostile towards democracy, a calculated hypocritical voice. It seemed as if every adult Black person in South Carolina knew of Thurmond's sexual indiscretions, as did a number of whites, including members of his own family. This writer became aware of this story while a freshman in college. It had been on the grapevine for the better part of forty years. The Strom Thurmond affair is a part of the lore, the crazy quilt complexity of southern "etiquette" involving Blacks and whites; this attraction-repulsion syndrome baffles many northerners. A definition for this drama is beyond category.

Resistance to the transformation of southern life that was ignited by the *Brown* decision cannot be overstated. There were a few moderate white voices; courageous journalists such as Harry Ashmore of Arkansas, Hodding Carter of Mississippi, Harry Golden of North Carolina, and the powerful voice of Lillian Smith, standout. It was Lillian Smith of Clayton, Georgia who wrote <u>Killers of the Dream</u> (1948), a book which shook the South with its strong antisegregationist message. Otherwise, the sing-song voices of politicians and preachers filled the airways and the press of the South with venom, using every foul means at hand – from distortions of Holy Scripture to pseudoscience – to thwart human progress; the civil rights movement was called "a Communist front," the civil rights movement was "a Zionist plot"; the NAACP was run by "subversives" and "the Jews from New York"; "our niggras go north and come back with funny ideas." This was a part of the commonplace rhetoric of southern resistance.

Rosa Parks and Martin Luther King, among other civil rights leaders, had done workshops with Miles Horton of the Highlander Folk School in the backwaters of Tennessee in the 1950s. The Highlander Folk School was comprised of a small group of committed progressive white southerners who were among the earliest whites of that time to support the Black struggle for social justice. They too, were labeled reds or pinkos or race traitors who influenced Parks and King to resist the doctrine of white supremacy. And then, the overt violence across the South: Clinton, Tennessee, and scores of other places erupted in the bombing of schools.

"Dynamite Hill" was a neighborhood in Birmingham, Alabama, where a series of bombings took place targeting Black middle class homes; this was a fruitless attempt to intimidate the likes of the fearless leader of the Birmingham Integrationist Movement, the Reverend Fred Shuttlesworth.

Perhaps the most confused act of resistance to the flood tide that *Brown v. Board* had let loose was the southern politician's funding of the construction for building new schools in the Black community in order to preserve Jim Crow. There was also the proliferation of new Christian white schools all over the South, and the complete shutdown of school systems, in certain counties in the South, in order to preserve white privileges. All of this and more had resulted from the impact of Brown. To this, Martin Luther King countered with the majesty of a soaring eagle:

> We will win the goal of freedom in Birmingham and all over
> America, because the goal of America is freedom. Scorned
> and abused though we may be, our destiny is tied to the des-
> tiny of America. Before the pilgrims landed, we were here.
> Before the pen of Thomas Jefferson etched the majestic
> words of the Declaration of Independence across the pages
> of history, we were here. For nigh three centuries our fore-
> bearers labored without wages. They made cotton king, they
> built the homes of their masters while suffering gross injus-
> tice and shameful humiliation, and yet out of a bottomless
> vitality they continued to thrive and develop. If the inex-
> pressible cruelties of slavery could not stop us then, the
> opposition we now face will surely fail.

"All Deliberate Speed" would serve to blunt any meaningful efforts to integrate for more than a decade. As Malcolm X, the militant Muslim minister, was fond of pointing out, "integration is not taking place, neither south nor north." After the official dismantling of school segregation, the term integration was either a broad amorphous one or a more definitive one, meaning integration was a one-way street; Black people crossing over to wherever whites were became the most compelling meaning. Black people being absolved into white institutions was not questioned by very many Black people. Those who did were thought to be unappreciative of "racial progress." A discussion of the sharing of resources rarely entered the discourse. The fundamental reality of the obscenely unshared power relationship between Blacks and whites never took root. Power automatically went with whiteness. The mythical belief in "race" overshadowed the core reality of the question; whites had all of the power and Black people had none, political, economic, or otherwise. A reasonable solution would seem to be a just system of power sharing. It was not until the slogan "Black power" emerged in the mid-1960s (outside of the Nation of Islam), that some Black advocates began to rethink the unchallenged integrationist position. Was the High Court's matter-of-fact assertion that Black schools were "inherently inferior" too narrow an interpretation of the complexity of human life? Was not such language really a euphemism for the continued dominance of white supremacy? Were the deplorable conditions that Black children endured in dilapidated schools a matter of genes, or the misuse of power? Such questions now linger. "Race" is neither a personal nor human reality, but a political reality: "The mind doesn't take its complexion from the skin." "All deliberate speed" had no doubt perverted the essential meaning of *Brown v. Board*. Despite this, the decision made for a number of new issues to come about as a result of its immeasurable impact: Busing, decentralization, open schools, alternative schools, home schools, voucher programs and charter schools are all, in some way, related to *Brown*. And most are relatively new realities in the field of education. Few of these existed before *Brown*. There are a plethora of other unnamed programs, system of changes, tests, and labels for certain students that could be gathered here. And the end of the road seems nowhere near.

Epilogue

The late Ralph McGill was editor of the powerful Atlanta Constitution and leader of the moderate voices of the white South. His southern heritage notwithstanding, he had this to say regarding the meaning of the Supreme Court Decision and its implications for social change in America:

> *All this means that attainment of civil rights is only a means to the more distant end – the long-term harvest of social, political and economic reforms made possible by the possession and use of those rights. Planning and foresight, which will enlist all Americans of whatever racial background, to build a stronger nation of commitment and belief is the opportunity offered by days and nights that move toward us. If we miss this second opportunity – 100 years after the first – it is unlikely we will have another.*

We must also be mindful of a caveat, if not a prophecy, from one of the students of those stormy days, Kwame Ture (aka Stokely Carmichael), former Chairperson of the Student Nonviolent Coordinating Committee. He foretells that "integration is but a form of subterfuge for the maintenance of white supremacy."

The boundless wisdom of Frederick Douglass puts forth the challenge to all Americans, which confronts their moral fortitude:

> *There is no Negro problem. The problem is whether the American people have honor enough, loyalty enough, and patriotism enough, to live up to their own Constitution.*

The question is now whether Americans, as a people, have emotionally, spiritually, politically, and morally matured enough to accept the challenge to complete the unfinished work of American political democracy. Only time will tell.

There is perhaps no sounder way to close this discussion, than by calling on the prophetic vision of W. E. B. DuBois, to define the long-term meaning of this journey towards freedom, which is always tied to identity and destiny – that is to say, we are bound in the long-term meaning of the struggle to make life anew:

One thing alone I charge you

as you live, believe in life!

always human beings will live

and progress to greater, broader, and fuller life.

The only possible death is

to lose belief in this truth,

simply because the great

end comes slowly,

because time is long.

W. E. B. DuBois

NOTES

From Slavery to Freedom
    John Hope Franklin

Before the Mayflower
    Lerone Bennett, Jr.

In Struggle, the Story of the Student Nonviolent
Coordinating Committee
    Claybourn Carson

The Strange Career of Jim Crow
    C. Vann Woodward

Freedom's Daughter
    Lynne Olson

Thurgood Marshall: American Revolutionary
    Juan Williams

The Road to Brown
    Video: A film from California News Reel / A
    Presentation of the University of Virginia

Eyes on the Prize
    Blackside Video Production

The Unsteady March
    Phillip A. Klinkner & Rogers M. Smith

All Deliberate Speech
    Charles J. Ogletree, Jr.

"King Leopold's Soliloquy"
    Mark Twain

White Supremacy
    George Fredrickson

Ebony Magazine, May 2004

Silent Covenants
    Derrick Bell

About the Author

Mahmoud El-Kati

Mahmoud El-Kati is a lecturer, writer, and commentator on the African American experience. He specializes in African American history and is an advocate of the concepts of ethnicity and community in the U.S.

El-Kati is a former lecturer at Macalester College in St. Paul, Minn. His articles, essays, and reviews deal with a variety of issues including the "myth of race," Ebonics, gang activity, African Americans, sports, and other issues. They have appeared in several newspapers and publications including the *New York Times*, *St. Paul Pioneer Press*, *Star Tribune*, *Insight News*, *The Spokesman*, and *The Nigerian Times*.

He is a frequent commentator through a variety of print and electronic media locally and nationally. Locally, he is a board member of KMOJ radio, a community-run station, and nationally, he is a regular columnist for *Insight News*, a Twin Cities newspaper.

El-Kati teaches courses on the history of Blacks in the United States, American social movements, sports and the African American community, and the social history of jazz and Afro-American folklore. He also teaches the African American experience class at North High School in Minneapolis. In addition, El-Kati teaches classes across the community and conducts workshops for educators in the Midwest region.

He is cofounder and director of the annual Pan-African Conference at Minnesota State University, which over the last 24 years has featured discussions on African thought throughout the Diaspora.

El-Kati is a founding member of the following institutions and organizations: The African and African-American Department at the University of Minnesota; the Community Investment Fund and the Pan African Community Endowment (both are grant-making conduits to grassroots community projects); Stairstep Foundation, a philanthropic and economic development institution for community empowerment; New Century I Cooperative Lending Fund, designed to create financial assets to make loans accessible to members of the community; and CommUniversity, a self-help education program that brings academic lectures to community life.

El-Kati is actively involved in community organizations such as MARCH and the Minneapolis-based Stairstep Foundation. He is a recipient of the National Association of Black Storytellers' Zora Neale Hurston Award, given to people whose scholarly historical writings preserve the culture and tradition of Africans and African Americans in America. He also recently received a Sankofa Award from the Stairstep Foundation for his longtime and unwavering commitment to and work with the Twin Cities' African American community.

El-Kati was a U.S. representative to the 1999 PANAFest Conference held in Acraa, Ghana, West Africa. PANAFest is an International biannual gathering of scholars, cultural workers, and artists, where he presented a paper at the symposium on Africans in the Diaspora.

El-Kati is a graduate of Wilberforce University in Ohio.